PAST WINNERS OF THE
U.S. OPEN AND THE BRITISH OPEN
in anagram form (answers other end of book)

got weirdos

I snuck jackal

tiger fee soon

no trench toy

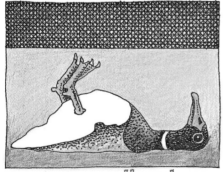

prone mallard

ALWAYS BE BEAUTIFUL

swan

GOLF FAIRWAY FABLES BY SIMON DREW

ONE HIT WONDER

ANTIQUE COLLECTORS' CLUB

to Caroline
and
all struggling golfers

©2013 Simon Drew
World copyright reserved

ISBN 978-1-905377-69-5

British Library Cataloguing-in-Publication Data
A catalogue record for this book is available from the British Library

Printed in China
for the Antique Collectors' Club Ltd., Woodbridge, Suffolk

INTRODUCTION :

LITTLE KNOWN FACTS ABOUT THE HISTORY OF GOLF

1 "Fore", a warning to other golfers, is in fact a contraction of "forgive me my trespasses".

2 A 'birdie' was the word chosen for a score one under par because they'd already used 'eagle' and 'albatross' and they couldn't think of any other bird names.

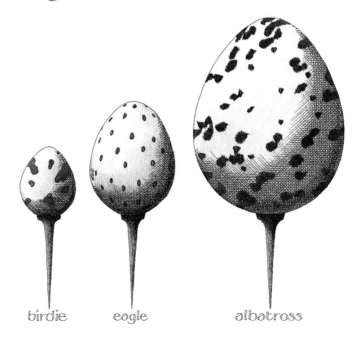

birdie   eagle   albatross

3. A golf ball left in a glass of coke overnight will disappear.

fig. A
(before)

fig. B
(after)

4 The Iron Curtain is, in fact, nothing to do with golf.

5 It was originally thought that golf was invented when a certain Dougal McDougal used a stick to hit a stone at a deer when he got bored deerstalking. This is not true. (He actually invented darts when he became bored while fly-fishing.)

6. The 'green' at the end of each hole is actually named after the first groundsman Charles Green who became known as Capability Green.

7. Neil Armstrong played the first golf shot on the moon (though he was disqualified for not paying the green-fee).

8 If one has planned a picnic as part of the day's golf, it is generally frowned on to use one of the greens to lay out the rug and delicacies.

One should be careful of thunderstorms when playing golf as it can result in damp sandwiches.

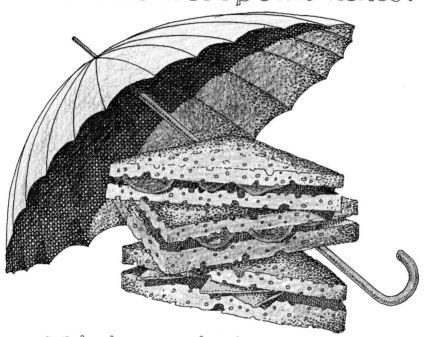

9 This is a variation of golf that never caught on:

tee for two

Vermeer's 'Golf-shoe cleaner'

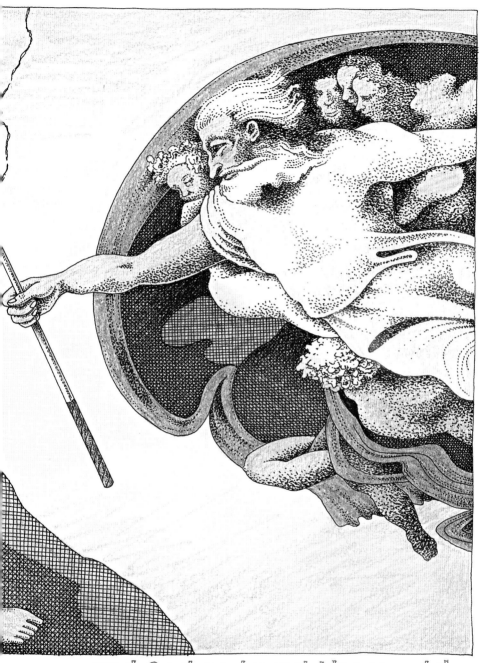

and God so loved the world
that he gave it golf.

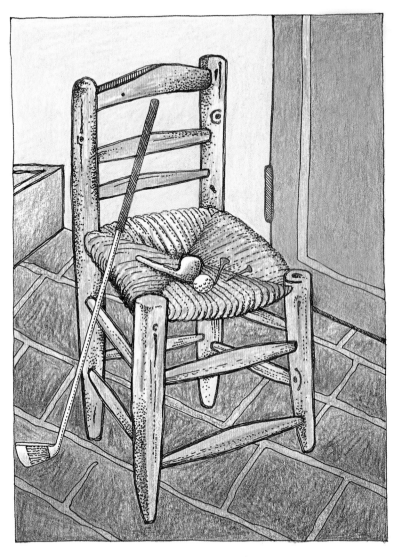

van golf

.... whatever the weather, Leonard
never missed a chance to practise.

Everyone wanted to play with Botticelli
when he had his caddy with him.

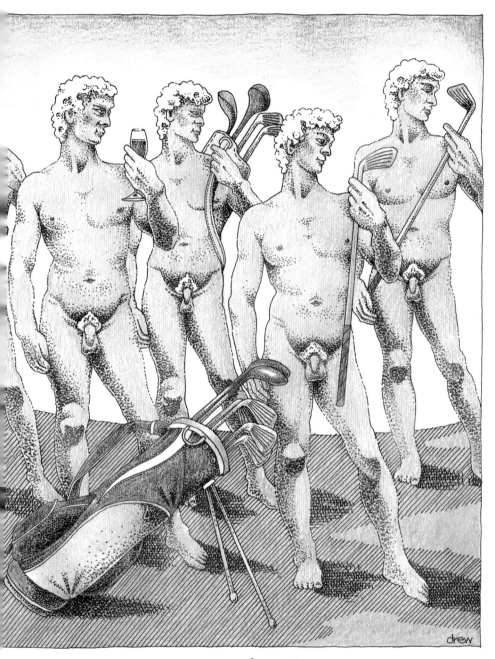

MICHELANGELO'S GOLF CLUB

the missed putt

BIRDS OF THE GOLF COURSE

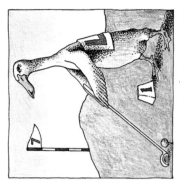

learner driver

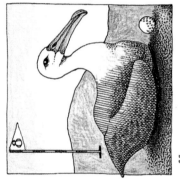

albatross

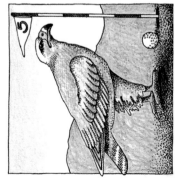

eagle

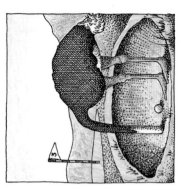

sand trap bird

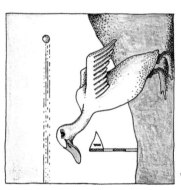

duck

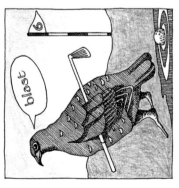

grouse

UNUSUAL GOLF HAZARDS

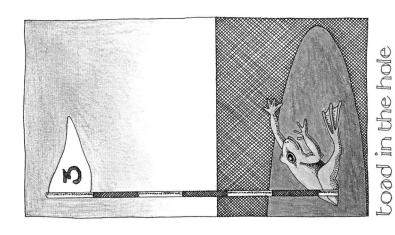

3

toad in the hole

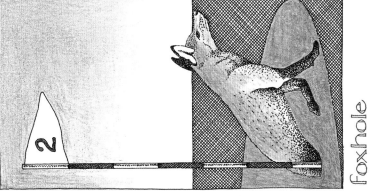

2

foxhole

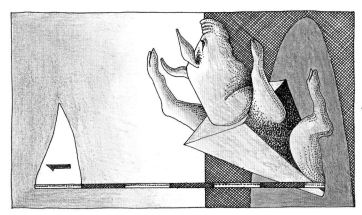

1

square pig
in a round hole

SPOT THE DIFFERENCE

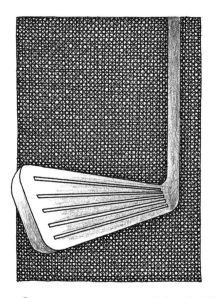

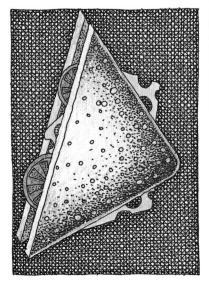

SAND WEDGE

SAND WIDGE

it took Edward years to perfect his swing

"Golf is a game in which a sphere
1·68 inches in diameter is placed on a
sphere 8000 miles in diameter. The
object is to hit the little sphere,
not the big one."

winston churchill

THE BALLAD OF THE LOST BALL

A Golfer's Fairy Tale

1

On a non-descript day
with everything grey
when cats can't be bothered with grins,
we were all feeling bored
and so, thank the Lord,
it's here where the story begins.

2
Don't be alarmed:
I think you'll be charmed
by the golfer, who's really a bird.
The first hole went well,
though the second was hell;
but see what he played on the third.

3

The shot was immense
(bounced over the fence)
and dropped in the mouth of a horse,
which ran in surprise
with gob-stopper eyes
and coughed the ball back on the course.

4.
There's less to report
on the next bit of sport
til the ninth when his drive hit a bus;
(the people inside
were so frightened they cried)
but the ball was returned without fuss.

5

More drama ensued
when a man in the nude
came wandering onto the green.
He was ushered away
and was last heard to say:
"Please wait: I've been sent by the Queen."

6

Then the ball found a hole
that was made by a mole
on the fourteenth: it just trickled in.
Was this velvety beast
much disturbed? Not the least.
So it pushed the ball nearer the pin.

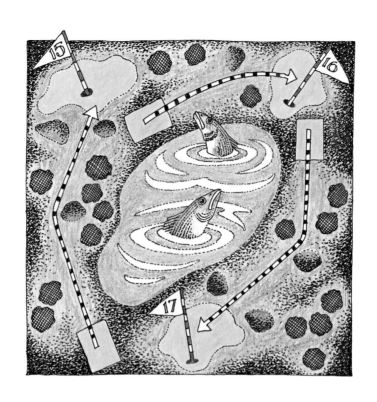

7

So now, slightly vexed,
it's on to the next :
the three holes that circle the lake
With all fingers crossed
no balls will be lost
as long as the ice doesn't break.

8

The ultimate goal
was our hero's last hole –
the eighteenth: the scene of disgrace.
With the mightiest swing
he hammered the thing:
it seemed it might finish in space . . . .

9

The ball bounced away
to a castle, they say,
where a maid, Cinderella, scrubbed floors.
She'd bleach any stains
and unblock the drains
and a hundred and one other chores.

10

Though stuck in a groove
her luck could improve,
for a prince had appeared at her gate.
Her beauty, he'd heard,
was that of a bird
and he hoped he could alter her fate.

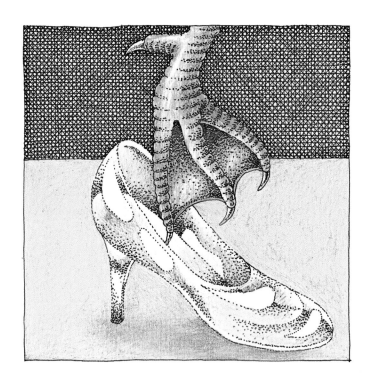

11

The prince took the stairs
like a deer chased by bears
to give Cinderella a prize.
Presenting glass shoes
and, with no time to lose,
he begged her to try them for size.

12

But the ball in this farce
then shattered the glass
and knocked out her handsome
                          young friend.

For Cinders, no chance
to go to the dance
though the ball came to her in the end.

....from mark twain

golf is a good walk ruined

"The reason the pro tells you
to keep your head down is
so you can't see him laughing."

Phyllis Diller

The putter is a club designed to hit the ball halfway to the hole.

Don't drink & drive.
Don't even putt.

GREEN PEACE

Is my friend in the bunker
or is the bastard on the green?

My wife says that if I don't give up golf,
she'll leave me.
I'm really going to miss her.

When you are putting
well, you are a
good putter.
When your opponent
is putting well,
he has a good putter.